For 1-25-98

Louise
Happy Birthday!
with Love-
Eileen

True Friends

By
Evelyn L. Beilenson

Illustrated by
Ms. Murray Callahan

PETER PAUPER PRESS, INC.
WHITE PLAINS, NEW YORK

Text copyright © 1996
Peter Pauper Press, Inc.
202 Mamaroneck Avenue
White Plains, NY 10601
Illustrations copyright © 1996
Murray Callahan
All rights reserved
ISBN 0-88088-797-4
Printed in China
7   6   5   4   3

✿✿✿

True Friends

✿✿✿

True Friends

Aren't you lucky when you have True Friends? You know, people who:

- show signs of aging at the same rate you do.

- are on time (most of the time).

- listen when no one else hears.

- make going to the mall seem like an adventure.

  We hope that, when leafing through this book, you will realize that you do indeed have many True Friends.

  E. L. B.

True Friends...

remember your
birthday but
forget your age.

True Friends...

hear your old
stories with
new ears.

True Friends...

always have
words of
encouragement.

True Friends...

are the
best mirrors.

True Friends . . .

share memories
of the good old days—
and dreams of
days to come.

True Friends . . .

help you see
the forest before
the trees.

True Friends...

show signs of aging
at the same rate
you do.

True Friends. . .

keep your secrets
under lock
and key.

True Friends . . .

make the gift of
self more precious
than a diamond.

True Friends...

———— ◦◦◦ ————

share food for
thought and thoughts
of food!

True Friends. . .

light up your life
when you're in
the dark.

$\mathcal{T}rue\ \mathcal{F}riends$. . .

know laughter can
be the best
medicine.

True Friends...

⸻ ❧ ⸻

allow you
to think
out loud.

True Friends . . .

read you
like a book.

True Friends...

**are on time
(most of the time).**

True Friends...

are there for you
at every turn
in the road.

True Friends...

like fine wine,
get better
with time.

True Friends...

find comfort
in the little things.

True Friends...

listen when
no one else hears.

True Friends...

— ⁃ ⁃ ⁃ — ⦿ — ⁃ ⁃ ⁃ —

will tell you
when an outfit
is not "you."

True Friends...

are not offended
when you put
them on "hold."

True Friends . . .

**don't always
agree.**

True Friends...

love you for
who you are.

True Friends . . .

pick you up
when you're
feeling down.

True Friends . . .

remind you to
have a sense of humor
about yourself.

True Friends...

enjoy sharing
special talents.

True Friends . . .

see you through
love lost and
weight gained.

True Friends...

like good health,
are even more valued
when they are lost.

True Friends...

—————— ⚬⚬ ——————

help you stretch
your mind as well as
your body.

True Friends...

make going to
the mall seem like
an adventure.

True Friends . . .

are never far apart
even though oceans
may come between them.

True Friends . . .

share good advice,
recipes, and bargains.

True Friends...

share gossip
and never tell.

True Friends...

help you when
the going gets tough.

True Friends...

⁓⁓⁓

share a
philosophy of life.

True Friends...

share your thoughts
and dreams.

True Friends...

weather the storm
in search of
the rainbow.